Tell Her Yes

Ann Farley

A Publication of The Poetry Box®

Poems ©2022 Ann Farley
All rights reserved.

Editing & Book Design by Shawn Aveningo Sanders
Cover Design by Shawn Aveningo Sanders
  (with images licensed under Creative Commons
  layered over original watercolor by Ann Farley)
Author Photo by Kevin Farley

No part of this book may be reproduced in any manner whatsoever without permission from the author, except in the case of brief quotations embodied in critical essays, reviews and articles.

ISBN: 978-1-956285-04-8
Printed in the United States of America.
Wholesale distribution via Ingram.

Published by The Poetry Box®, April 2022
Portland, Oregon
https://ThePoetryBox.com

*For my mother,
Rae Daley*

*Thank you for giving me
the gift of travel and the opportunity
to learn about this beautiful world,
its people, creatures, and cultures.*

Poems

7	|	Flight
8	|	Love Song for Rain
9	|	I Am the River
10	|	At the Watering Hole
11	|	Bare Legs on Warm Wood
13	|	Early Morning in Dufur
14	|	Window
15	|	On the Sunset, Eastbound
16	|	Of Crocodiles
17	|	For a Glass of Water
18	|	Good Dirt
19	|	Dahlias
21	|	Visiting Hours During the Pandemic
22	|	Room #209
23	|	On the River
24	|	summit
27	|	they talk to me about dying
29	|	Mourning
30	|	With the Minus Tide
31	|	Taking Turns
32	|	On the Way to Tataouine
33	|	Buzzed
34	|	Mining
35	|	Check the Feeder
37	|	Refuge
38	|	Botany Lesson
39	|	Just Add Water

Flight

Don't you wish now and then
you could hold open a book
spine splayed, pages fluttering,
heft it above your head
so the pages turn to wings
as you clutch the covers,
front and back,
and let it lift you
up, up, up?

Love Song for Rain

There is that moment
    on the path through the woods
        when you stop to listen

to the rain as it falls
    in dainty drops on brown leaves
        still clinging to branches,

then rolls and collects,
    surrenders in hushed thuds
        to the ground. A song sparrow

hunkered in the bramble
    gives a tentative trill,
        waits, warbles again

his unwavering want. Behind you,
    in the thick basket of brush,
        another answers.

I Am the River

~ for Kevin

This is how we are, like the bay
    where the Salmon River tangos
        through tall marsh, Sitka snags and driftwood,
            before spilling into the Pacific.

        At our best we are an expanse of blue,
        a shallow of nurture, home
    to gulls and eagles, herons and harbor seals,
fish and frogs, dragonflies like jewels.
Wind bent trees are shade and shelter.

At our worst we are a flat, muddy expanse,
    drained and wanting. Our murky underbelly
        exposes long silences and storm damage,
            the unexpected seasons of drought.

            Still, we flow on, curling and settling
        in comfortable furrows, filling, emptying,
    filling again. We weather frothy unrest
and cold, gray mist, await the return
of sun and stars and ripe moon guidance.

I am the river, a coursing flow, spits
    of anger and washes of calm, cool water,
    and you are the shores of my containment,
        the earth and rock and sand.

At the Watering Hole

Terrapins sense the approach first,
slip necks under helmet-green shells,
backpedal down mud bank, slide into murk.

Gray heron on granite perch
spreads wings, lifts off and away.
Elephants are coming.

At water's surface, pink ears swivel and flick,
nostrils flare, eyes blink as hippos turn
in unison. Three adult elephants,

a young one tucked between them, thud
a worn path to shallow access.
As lead elephant swings and dips her trunk

into the muddy pool, a hippo snorts and rises,
her heft a wall between her calf and threat.
Mouth agape, teeth bared, feet set,

I am that hippo, as is every other female
who has ever born an offspring.

Bare Legs on Warm Wood
A Visit to Stony Brook Wildlife Sanctuary

That early August afternoon
I was new to motherhood and had given up
    trying to get anything done,
        the baby just three months old,
        the baby we bottle fed after every attempt at nursing,
            who cried out of hunger and need,
            who slept in twenty minute fits of exhaustion
                and woke wanting more, more, more,
            who, we would learn,
                was tongue-tied and couldn't suckle,
I took the baby to a nearby nature park
    of flat paths lined with low rock walls
    and a maze of boardwalks
        through marshes and ponds,
strapped him in the stroller and rolled,
    let him fuss to maple trees and painted turtles,
        bullfrogs and blue jays,
    let his hiccuping squawk
        skip like a stone across water's surface,
but the moment we stepped on the path
    under a confetti of light falling through branches
        and the lapping murmur of water
he was quiet,
    swiveled his head to look this way and that
        as the stroller wheels thrummed
            down gray weathered boards,
    my swollen breasts responded to rhythmic rolling,
        spilled two rounds of wet on my T shirt,
and by the time I found a shady spot with a view
    of mallards and a great blue heron,

[. . .]

he was asleep,
>	lulled by the green scent of duck weed and reeds,
>		even the boards gave off
>			a whiff of familiar comfort,
so I sat beside my son,
>	folded bare legs on warm wood,
>		looked out across sky blue water
>		and watched a dragonfly land on a lily pad
>	in that moment of doing absolutely nothing.

Early Morning in Dufur

7 AM and a dull yellow CAT, a grader, rumbles to life
in the lot next to the Balch Hotel. Two orange
and white traffic cones, set on poles flanking the snout
of the cab, look like ears on a beast.

When my autistic son was nine, he took
horseback riding lessons. His instructor said, *See
the space between the ears? That's your windshield.
Steer with the reins.*

One day my son's favorite horse, a big, black
thoroughbred named Roscoe, was gone, given up
as a gift to the instructor's now ex. My son
balled his fists, kicked the stable door.
I froze. There is no telling what an upset autistic boy
will do. But that was the end of it.

At least, that was the end of it for my son. I stand
twenty years later watching a grader idle
and I'm back in that barn, vibrating
like the CAT's engine. Braced.

Window

Move the woman with dementia to a window.
Ask her what she sees.
Go with her.
Tell her yes.

On the Sunset, Eastbound

We leave earlier than necessary
to go to the neurologist's office.
I lie about the appointment time.
Nothing slows an old man
like being rushed.

We snake the sloping curves
to the tunnel into Portland, traffic thick
but moving, until, abruptly, it isn't.
I calculate the distance left,
chances of finding parking near an elevator,
hallways we need to walk,
how often he might shuffle to a stop
to ask a question,
gaze out a window.

Time trickles while we sit
like rocks in a river.
I am careful not to fidget or sigh.
But he leans forward,
examines the cars, the hillsides,
the tall trees, the downward twist of the road.
Then he focuses on me. His eyebrows arch.
He says, *This is good.*
I know this place.

Of Crocodiles

I don't see the crocodile snap one of the egrets
from the bank. Instead I see, where a moment before
two had been strutting and pecking at water's edge,

a single egret flutter a jitterbug on brown mud bank
and the quick roil of water's surface smooth over.
Is it not a universal wish to die in one's sleep?

Florence didn't fret about crocodiles or a jarring end,
but the very notion of a long linger had her plotting.
If she could figure out how to swing her legs

over balcony banister, she'd jump in a heartbeat.
No idle threat. Eight stories up, concrete landing pad
below. Don't do that, I said. It would be messy.

In the end, her end came quickly, as planned,
on schedule, a prescribed cocktail of eternal sleep.
Funny I should stand on this man-made dike

above a sluggish, muddy pond hiding who knows what
and think of Florence all these years after the fact.
The lone egret ventures closer and closer to the water.

She will have to wade in to feed on minnows and frogs.
She will have to hope the crocodile has had his fill.

For a Glass of Water

I'm at the kitchen sink filling a glass of water
for my father-in-law when I catch a flash
of red out the window. There, at the base of the Hawthorne tree

a red-breasted sapsucker drills neat rows of holes
in the trunk near a cluster of new shoots I need to trim.
One more thing to do, tend the yard, cut back

that junk tree full of thorns and a powerful zest
for reckless growth. But in the spring
it is a wedding veil of tiny white blossoms,

and in fall, red berries entice flocks of robins and cedar
    waxwings,
who feast on fermented fruit and flap silly, branch to branch
and across our lawn. The sapsucker visits year round,

but I haven't noticed him recently. I've been too busy
caring for my father-in-law, after the effects of dehydration
on body and mind nearly drained him of life.

What was I doing? Oh yes,
getting a glass of water, preparing his lunch.
Maybe this afternoon, or tomorrow, I'll trim that tree.

And when I kneel down with my clippers,
I will share space where a wild bird perched.

Good Dirt

~ for Suzanne

Callouses like pebbles dig into her feet.
She winces her way to her chair.

Now, she says, *it's my knees too.*
She waves a bony hand.

Years ago you told me
people are ready to die when they hurt.

She taps the blue topaz in her ring.
See this? It came from Earth.

My Earth. Where I will soon go.
Do you hear me? I am happy

to return to Earth, to lie in good dirt,
to look up at gray sky.

Let it rain down on me.
I am not afraid.

Let Earth press me into something new.
Or just take me back.

I hand her a glass of cranberry juice, red
like rubies. *Ah,* she says, *thank you.*

Dahlias

I don't want to arrive too early
for the meeting at the rehab center,
so I go to my garden,
cut all the dahlias I have. Four.
They flop around my Goodwill vase.

I cut lemon balm, rose campion, lavender
and two red hot pokers, enough to fill.
Jan is terminal. Rehab seems beside the point.
I've been a caregiver for years,
so the family asked me to come, to talk.
I bring absurdly happy pink dahlias
with yellow centers.
You can't go to a place like that empty-handed.

Jan reaches, but hasn't the strength
to hold the vase. We go to a conference room,
I place the dahlias on the table.
Jan's daughter moves them aside
so we can see each other.

I ask, *What would you like to know?*
I'm no adviser.
I'm there to say what needs to be said:
facility, home, agency, bed bath, morphine,
bed sores, palliative care, hospice.

Her daughter asks, *Mom,
what do you want?*

Jan says, *Comfort.*
She gazes at the vase.

Comfort. No pain.
She is beyond sentences.

Ice cream, she says.
Dahlias.

Visiting Hours During the Pandemic

What am I doing here? What am I doing here?
He asks, but meaning is mumbled behind his mask.
We sit six feet apart in the sun by the facility's front door.
Cars, delivery trucks, people — our words can't compete.

He asks, but meaning is mumbled behind his mask.
By *here*, does he mean what is he still doing *alive?*
Cars, delivery trucks, people — our words can't compete.
His mask slips as he reaches both arms out to me.

By *here*, does he mean what is he still doing *alive?*
His neck is white stubble. Has he forgotten how to shave?
His mask slips as he reaches both arms out to me.
He doesn't understand why I don't return his embrace.

His neck is white stubble. Has he forgotten how to shave?
We sit six feet apart in the sun by the facility's front door.
He doesn't understand why I don't return his embrace.
What am I doing here? What am I doing, here?

Room #209

It's a clear, plate glass window
double-paned per building code
four-foot square center pane, flanked

by two long rectangular windows,
screens shut per COVID code
or interior temperature control.

White sticker slapped mid-window
on the outside for room identification
black perma-marker, #209

thin film of grit like a filter. Three nurses' aids
in protective gear move like ghosts in shadow,
lift him from bed to wheelchair.

They struggle to dress him
fold his body into the vinyl seat, hold him
upright as they wheel him to the window.

No foot rests, his right foot drags, catches
on the floor. He grimaces.
I want to cry, I don't want to cry.

Can he hear me through this window
this clear portal, this solid barrier between us?
His head hangs, he cannot see me.

I press my hand against the cold
grimy window, as if I can will
glass to return to silica,

as if this window might shift to something
like sand, porous and forgiving,
as if he feels my touch.

On the River

After weeks of saying no
she didn't want her hair washed
she was dying, wasn't she

just going to be put in the dirt
what did it matter if her hair was dirty
after the night she dreamed

she sat along the Columbia
feasting on huckleberries
and salmon roasted on a wood fire

she said *I might as well have my hair washed*
her daughter and I gathered towels
got to it before she changed her mind

cradled her head like a newborn
this chance to touch and tend
this branch over the river

caught before the moment swept away
we eased her back to rest
her long, damp gray wisps

fanned across her pillow
like river grass in the shallows
combed by a gentle current

her daughter called to her brother, her husband
come see mom, come see
she's so beautiful

afloat in her raft of a bed
we stood on the shore by her side
watching her drift down river

summit

what you will need:

pillows, pillows of every sort
to lift and cradle your head, support neck and shoulders
tuck against your left, then right side, and back again
shifting your weight to stave off bed sores
another pillow between or beneath your knees

the oblong pillow your aunt cross-stitched when you were born
fits nicely under your ankles
keeps your heels from pressing into the mattress
keeps the skin and soft tissue from breaking down

nightgowns, pretty ones, but not too many
plush towels, large and small
something soft, like your old, one-eared stuffed bear
or the blue bandanna you bought when you were seventeen
to hold when the need to clutch something becomes too much

bed pads
disposable undergarments
wet wipes
a plastic bucket or bin
you just never know, the body does what the body does
gloves

let me bathe your brow, cool the damp back of your neck
let me wash your face, chest, the soft underpart of your arms
let me tend to the whole of your body

lotion, as much for you as for others
so they may hold your hands and rub gentle circles
into your palms, fingers and nail-beds
along the veins of memories held in your arms

sheets and blankets, stacks of them
you will be dry and clean and warm
just roll a little this way and that
you don't have to get up to have your bedding changed

a cobalt blue vase filled with yellow roses on the nightstand
music, perhaps flute or harpsichord

drugs, the drugs of sweet dreams
the effortless rhythmic puff of oxygen
you won't hurt at all, no worries, no pain, nothing but comfort
    and ease
just rest, sleep will come and go
we'll talk, if you want to talk, in the moments when you are
    awake
I will sit and wait, we will pick up
where we left off
a notebook and pen to keep track of it all

tissues
mouth swabs and lip balm and bendy straws
anything you want to eat or drink
a fresh ripe strawberry, mocha-chip ice cream, scrambled eggs
buttered toast with cinnamon sugar
fresh squeezed orange juice
soon the body will forget about the stomach
and focus effort on heart and lungs
all you will want then is a little water
if that

what, you wonder, will become of all this
of you, of us, at the summit?
you just go on
we stay behind and watch
then gather up and cart away what wasn't needed

[. . .]

you keep going
we return to where we have always been
but we will have been to the thin place
we will have hovered there
a moment with you
and nothing will ever be the same

we will have to relearn this place
the shock of it all
the car will need gas and maybe new tires
the phone will ring
bills will need to be paid, the grass mowed, the laundry done
a child will want dinner
there will be a trip to the grocery store with its excess and noise
    and light
alarm clocks will ring and time will tick on and it will take so long
to figure out how to be here again
without you

they talk to me about dying

many are ready to go
their children don't want to hear it
this great relief in reviewing life
readying home and mind for leaving
little left to fear or want
except to be heard
fully
by someone, anyone

I am the hired help
I do laundry, change beds
cook meals, clean the kitchen
I scrub backs, wipe bottoms, rinse hair
thread arms through sleeves
roll socks on swollen feet
I brew tea
I sit at a table and listen

they tell me of affairs and abortions
their father's depression
the flood that erased the family farm
fleeing an abusive spouse
being hit with a hairbrush by their mother
surviving polio, while a sister didn't
a son who molested a daughter
the day they took their last drink
the child they lost
the child who was arrested
the child they disowned
regrets puddle around us

good memories surface, too
soaking in a spa in Japan
lakes swum, races won

[. . .]

the granddaughter who visits and plays piano
meeting and courting their spouse
the summer they taught their children to sail
the first home they owned
the horse they rode to school
the dog that followed them and waited

they ask if there's an afterlife
if I believe in God
if there's a heaven
if dying hurts

they tell me they are tired
they tell me they are at peace
they feel free to talk
in a way they have never talked before

I carry the secrets of the dead
long after —

Mourning

Grief knows no time,
comes and goes as it pleases.

Try to push it away,
box and shelve it,
busy it into the shadows,
but still it will come
on a hint of a breeze,
work its way in
and settle like dust, everywhere.

Or it will come in a cold gust,
a rushing whirl of twirling chaos,
a relentless, tree bending wind.

Just breathe, and breathe again.

Acknowledge its comings and goings
and accept its truths:
there is love tucked in sadness,
honor afloat in tears,
a thousand memories shared in a sigh.

Sometimes the best you can do
is nothing at all.

Sit with loss,
and let it be.

With the Minus Tide

You need not fear,
she will come and go like the tides,
curl around your feet like strands of kelp
slippery and cool, a glancing touch,
a gentle tickle before the eternal tug.

Her salt-stained breath carries
music the sky hears, harmonies mapped
in the clouds and drumming rain;
the sea and sky are like one,
vast slates washing and changing
time and again, a cycle of cleansing
and readying for what comes next.

She will relieve you
of the purple shells, amber agates,
gray driftwood scraps scrubbed smooth
with time and experience,
all that you carry but no longer need.

She will empty your pockets of cares
and sorrows, your earth-bound burdens,
gritty truths, apologies saved for later,
and leave in her morning wake
a vast, uncluttered expanse
of fine golden sand glinting a path,
her promise of ease and contentment.

Do not worry, she is patient,
she is kind, she will wait for you
whenever you are ready,
then she will gather and hold you,
carry you beyond all that you know,
to rock on the sure, steady waves
of deep blue-green peace.

Taking Turns

My friend goes first,
    walks half a dozen steps or more.
        I watch and wait, take my time,
            enter as she makes the first turn,
        curves back around. Curves are wide.
    Turns are tight. The cobble stones,
once burnt red and sky gray,
have aged and weathered
    closer to the color of dust.
        Hard to tell apart,
            I must watch each step, or risk
        veering into her lane.
    Head lowered, I study stones,
anticipate her course.
An oddly intimate act,
    sharing this planned garden
        of mindful meandering,
            a convoluted path to center.
    I want to time it so
    she has her moment,
unspools when she is ready,
not because I intrude.
    Moss like emeralds
        burbles between the stones,
            light through tree leaves
        marbles the way. Here is a weed,
    a tuft of grass. My friend and I
are separate, yet together,
winding and unwinding,
    following our course,
        giving each other space,
            casting shadows, crossing paths.
      A peace, like flute notes
    filtering through tall grass,
finds us where we began.

On the Way to Tataouine

When camels come down
to the thin line of road skirting
the purple shadowed Atlas Mountains,
stoop splay-legged
on faded pavement,
and swing long brown necks
to drink from mirage-like puddles
left by this morning's showering tease,
our driver stops,
rests his hands in robed lap,
watches and waits as if this delay
is one more call to prayer.

Buzzed

The buzzard doesn't hit the windshield
so much as swim across, talons skittering,
tail feathers fanned, a swooping rush

of black, white and rust-brown —
the driver and I fling arms up and duck.
The vehicle swerves, but there's no road,

no oncoming traffic, just flat hard-pack
where sand used to be and will come again.
The others in the backseat yell out,

want to know what's happening,
but the buzzard disappears as abruptly
as it came. The driver clasps his turban,

no longer shy and distant, flashes me
a wide-eyed smile. We both hoot a laugh.
He will go back to looking ahead,

fingering wooden prayer beads looped
on the steering wheel, but the sands
have shifted. The ride is smooth.

Mining

Forgiveness does not fall from the sky
like rain or sift out of fog to settle
like a net of droplets on your hair.
It is in the earth.
You have to dig for it.

You can squat by a river and pan,
let fine sediment wash downstream,
but what's left on the screen
at the end of the day can fool you.
It's not that easy.

Get a hold of a good shovel,
wear gloves and thick soled shoes.
You may hit rock, roots, clay,
a woolly mammoth femur,
although that's highly unlikely.

Sand may spill into the hole,
filling it while you work.
That's okay.
What you find may not be
what you thought you were seeking.

Forgiveness doesn't look like much.
It surfaces slowly, layers later
when your arms are pleasantly sore,
the sweat dribbling down your back
dries and your vision clears,

When you sit on an upturned bucket
and sigh, when the breadth and depth
of the hole no longer matters,
and the shovel handle fits
your palm like an old friend.

Check the Feeder

I don't see or hear the house finch
flutter into the dining room and perch
on the ladder-back chair,
but there he is, watching.

Was he, too, drawn in
by all the turquoise puzzle pieces
strewn on the table?

After months of semi-quarantine, I work
to manufacture some notion of joy,
wing away on imagination.

In the next room, the refrigerator hums.
The finch tilts his head, eyes me
with the same expression of curiosity
my father used when he focused on me,
a look that said, *Who are you?*
Where did you come from?

The finch hops, flaps and settles.
He tucks a wing, like a hand in a pocket.
His rose feathers on cheeks and chin,
chest and crown are the same color
my father flushed when he was angry
or when he laughed.

The finch interrupts, chirps,
What are you doing?
Go outside, don't mind the rain.
Check the feeder. Walk barefoot on a cushion
of pine needles under the Ponderosa.
Tend the earth. It will be okay, everything
that worries you now.

I get up, ease back white sheers,
and open the window.
My father left more than twenty years ago
in a morphine fog.
I don't know how the finch got in,
but when he wants to leave,
at least I have made his going easy.

Refuge

Take refuge in a forest of forgiveness.
Gather a quilt of moss, bunch berry and wood sorrel.
Lie down in a bed of ferns.
Fiddleheads unfurling brush away tears.
Wish upon trillium stars.

Venture narrow paths chiseled through brush
by mule deer and coyotes to patches
of huckleberries and thickets of cover.
Follow where trees give way to meadow's edge,
a carpet of sweet grass, tiger lilies, columbine,
buttercup, bluebells and promise.

Stow fears in hollows and under decaying logs,
lichen will tend to them in time.
Send regrets downstream on twigs and yellow leaves.

Let the twittering of chickadees, bush tits
and ruby-crowned kinglets trickle like splashes
of light through canopy cover.
Drum along with the downy.
Awaken to the mournful call of a great horned owl.

Old oaks offer shelter.
Douglas fir and cedar branches reach in embrace,
sweep a curl of comfort.
The darkest hour, find solace among Indian pipes,
pale clumps huddled in the understory shadows,
bell-shaped blossoms bowed in reverence.

Botany Lesson

Gazing at a flower, did you let yourself
land on yellow-dusted stamen
and travel a slender slope of filament

to bloom's fragrant center?
Did you journey further,
burrow into stem, slip down its hollow

to cool dirt and root's reach?
Is this how you learned you were
of the earth, connected to land and rain

and sun? Did you inhale light
and dark, touch tongue to dew?
Is this how you learned to count,

plucking petal after petal, loves me,
loves me not? Or how you learned
colors: periwinkle, violet, indigo, scarlet?

Is this how you studied shapes
and distance and how to dream?
Did a bee teach you

to hover, gather, lift and buzz,
to fly afield and explore
the bounty of blossoms?

Just Add Water

Mallard doesn't mind it's not a proper pond,
but a rain-swollen dip in a field
awaiting next season's planting of corn.
He is happy to flap and splash and paddle
in the fresh here and now, no matter
it will be a muddy bog in two days' time.
He will have taken leave, slapping
orange webbed feet across this surface,
a running start in his search for the next
glimmering welcome in a bountiful land.

Acknowledgments

Grateful acknowledgment is made to the editors of the publications who first printed these poems, sometimes as a different version.

Avocet: "At the Watering Hole"

Gobshite Quarterly: "Window," "Dahlias," and "Mining" (forthcoming)

Kosmos Quarterly: "Taking Turns"

Mom Egg Review VOX: "Bare Legs on Warm Wood"

pān/dé/mïk: "Visiting Hours During the Pandemic"

The Poeming Pigeon: From Pandemic to Protest: "Room #209"

RAIN Magazine: "Love Song for Rain," "Refuge," "With the Minus Tide," "I Am the River" (forthcoming), and "Good Dirt" (forthcoming)

Storms of the Inland Seas: Poems of Alzheimer's and Dementia Caregiving: "On the Sunset, Eastbound" (forthcoming)

Third Wednesday: "On the Way to Tataouine"

Timberline Review: "Early Morning in Dufur"

U.S. 1 Worksheets: "Of Crocodiles"

Verseweavers: "Just Add Water"

Willawaw Journal: "Buzzed"

The poem "summit" won third place for poetry in the Willamette Writers Kay Snow Award.

In Gratitude

Heartfelt thanks and appreciation for the support and encouragement of poet friends Dale Champlin, Kris Demien, Suzy Harris, Sherri Levine, and Vivienne Popperl.

Praise for *Tell Her Yes*

In *Tell Her Yes*, Ann Farley offers us lyric poems that speak the language of forgiveness, of patience, of humility and reverence. A number of these poems are about the natural world. A number are about her work giving palliative care. Given their compelling tone, all these poems are—in themselves—advocates for what's palliative. Calling us toward our better selves, this collection asks us to see ourselves as capable of sustained generosity and kindness. Farley's poems remind us that, like a beneficent river, "At our best we are an expanse of blue,/ a shallow of nurture," a haven for all whose lives touch ours.

—Paulann Petersen,
Oregon Poet Laureate Emerita

This poet is a caretaker, and the strength of this collection is appreciation, both for the natural world and for the fragile humans aging within it. In the title poem we are instructed "Move the woman with dementia to a window. Ask her what she sees. Go with her. Tell her yes." Ann Farley's poems say a passionate and just occasionally humorous *yes* to beauty, to loss, to acceptance.

—Penelope Scambly Schott,
author of *Sophia and Mister Walter Whitman*

Tell Her Yes, Ann Farley's debut chapbook, is a braided river flowing with 27 carefully-crafted poems that are both tender and wise, nurturing and consoling. Farley is a mother, caregiver, and nature-lover whose poems bear witness to some of life's most poignant moments. Whether she is taking her autistic son for a walk in a wildlife sanctuary ("Bare Legs on Warm Wood"), bringing dahlias to a woman in rehab who is beyond speaking in sentences ("Dahlias"), or serving as a family's sounding board, ("they talk to me about dying"), she fills her poems with pitch-perfect details that hit readers' hearts and minds with the authority of one who knows. And, indeed, these poems reveal their creator's firsthand knowledge of the journey into death as well as to the aliveness nature offers. When Farley writes in "Mourning," *Sometimes the best you can do/is nothing at all./ Sit with loss, and let it be,* readers of this stunning collection will be tempted to tell her yes.

—Carolyn Martin, Ph.D., poetry editor
of *Kosmos Quarterly: a journal for global transformation*

Well now, what a gorgeous collection of poems by Ann Farley! *Tell Her Yes* is as fresh as a day's rain in a dry season. Ann's prose poetry speaks of life viewed through the inanimate nature of ecology and the animated nature of being human. *Tell Her Yes* will bring to mind the beautiful poetics of the late great Mary Oliver and the humanness found in the works of Oregon poet, Jennifer Richter. For certain, there are images in these poems that will surely capture every reader's imagination. There is an old adage that says, "the proof is in the pudding." What a fine pudding Ann Farley has made for lovers of life described poetically.

—Emmett Wheatfall, poet
and author of *Our Scarlet Blue Wounds*

About the Author

Ann Farley, poet and caregiver, is happiest outdoors. She loves the beach, but she also enjoys an early morning walk in the park with her husband and dog. Her poems have appeared in *Timberline Review*, *Willawaw Journal*, *Verseweavers*, *The Poeming Pigeon*, *KOSMOS Quarterly*, *RAIN Magazine*, *Gobshite Quarterly* and others. Her poems have won first and third place in Oregon Poetry Association contests, and a third place Kay Snow Award for poetry. She lives in Beaverton, Oregon.

Email: annedf@comcast.net

Website: annfarleypoetry.com

IG: @farley2324

About The Poetry Box

The Poetry Box® is a boutique publishing company in Portland, Oregon, which provides a platform for both established and emerging poets to share their words with the world through beautiful printed books and chapbooks.

Feel free to visit the online bookstore (thePoetryBox.com), where you'll find more titles including:

The Catalog of Small Contentments by Carolyn Martin

World Gone Zoom by David Belmont

Protection by Michelle Lerner

Bee Dance by Cathy Cain

A Long, Wide Stretch of Calm by Melanie Green

Of the Forest by Linda Ferguson

Let's Hear It for the Horses by Tricia Knoll

Stronger Than the Current by Mark Thalman

Sophia & Mister Walter Whitman by Penelope Scambly Schott

What We Bring Home by Susan Coultrap-McQuin

The Kingdom of Birds by Joan Colby

Beneath the Gravel Weight of Stars by Mimi German

A Nest in the Heart by Vivienne Popperl

and more . . .